Chipping Norton T
Past & Prese

by
John Grantham

First Published 2007
with Poundstone Press
Jaffé and Neale
1 Middle Row
Chipping Norton
OX7 5NH

ISBN 9780955241017

The front cover :- shows the Town Hall as originally built, but before the bell tower was added, underneath as it is to-day.

The back cover :- shows the Town Hall before the disabled ramp was added, and underneath as it is to-day.

About the Author

John Grantham was born in Chipping Norton in 1937.

He was educated at the old British School in New Street, Church of England Boys School and at Chipping Norton Grammar School.

On leaving school he worked for GT Smith & Son, the TV & Electrical shop on High Street, and then served three years in the Royal Air Force as a Radar Operator, much of the time stationed in Hong Kong.

He joined Parker Knoll Furniture Ltd in 1962, and progressed through the company eventually becoming their Manufacturing Director, and working with them until retirement in 1997.

John served on Chipping Norton Borough / Town Council 1972-1983, and from 1994 until the present time. He also served on West Oxfordshire District Council from 1974 until 1977 and 1996-2000.

He was Mayor of Chipping Norton in 1976 and 1977.

He is a past Chairman of the Oxfordshire Association of Local Councils and the League of Friends of Chipping Norton & District War Memorial Hospital.

Along with John Hannis and Paul Burbidge he is a Life Trustee and Chairman of the Regulated Pasture, and Chairman of the Chipping Norton & District Volunteer Fire Brigade Fund.

His previous book The Regulated Pasture (a history of common land in Chipping Norton) published in 1997 reflected his keen interest in the towns past.

Chipping Norton Town Hall – past and present

From the time of the granting of a Charter on the 27th of February 1607, the town of Chipping Norton had been run by the "Corporation", consisting of two Bailiffs and twelve Burgesses, operating from the Guildhall.
In 1835 the Municipal Corporations Act came into force that put an end to the old charter, and from that date a Council consisting of a Mayor, four Aldermen and twelve Councillors governed the town.
The first Mayor was Alderman William Simkins Hitchman and the other members of the Council were:

Aldermen: William Fowler, Samuel Huckvale, Thomas Rolls.

Councillors: John Farwell, John Metcher, Edmund Woodman, Charles Phillips, George Fawler Tilsley, Henry Field Wilkins, Samuel Guy, John Ward, Richard Cooke, Robert Parsons, John Matthews and William Guy.

Every male person occupying a tenement for two years in respect of which rates had been paid was a Burgess and under the Act was entitled to vote by secret ballot at the election of Councillors.

By 1855 there were about 390 Burgesses who were entitled to vote.

Meetings were held quarterly in February, May, August and November, plus special meetings if there was urgent business needing to be discussed.

It was not long before the new Council decided that the Guildhall was inadequate for their purposes, and in 1841 a proposal was put forward to build a new Town Hall. This building would be more appropriate and would reflect the new "status" of the town; it would be sited where the Market Hall stood.

(The painting below is an impression of the Market place c 1825, artist unknown, and is now in the Caretaker's office)

The Town Hall was designed by GS Repton and cost in the region of £1800. It was built using local labour, the largest contractor being Meades & Company.

A public appeal was launched and soon over £600 was promised.

Mr JH Langston MP from Sarsden House offered a loan of £500 whilst not requiring any security. The remainder of the money was to come from selling off several pieces of wasteland in the town with permission to build houses. In addition, the old Market Hall was to be sold by Public Auction.

On the 7th February 1842 the old elm tree which had stood for over 200 years near to the Market Hall was sold at a Public Auction, and shortly after on 22nd March 1842 the Market Hall was sold in 3 lots:

(1) The covering of lead by weight
(2) Wood and timber
(3) Pillars and stone, which were bought by William Arkell for £160

One of the pillars of the original Market Hall can be seen on the west side of the Town Hall.
(See picture and plaque on page 4)

THE STONE AT THE BASE OF THIS COLUMN
FORMED PART OF THE OLD WAYSIDE CROSS
REMOVED FROM NEAR THIS SPOT BEFORE
THE BUILDING OF THE TOWN HALL.
THE UPPER PART IS ONE OF THE NINE
PILLARS OF THE OLD MARKET HALL WHICH
STOOD AT THIS APPROXIMATE POSITION
UNTIL 1842 WHEN IT WAS REMOVED
SO THAT THE PRESENT TOWN HALL
COULD BE BUILT.
RE-ERECTED HERE
1955

Buttercross column removed to Town Hall

One of the columns of Chipping Norton Buttercross, as the old Market Hall was called, now on the lawn on the south side of the Town Hall.

The market was pulled down to make room for the Town Hall when it was built about 115 years ago. Parts of the old building were sold, and one of the columns (there are believed to have been nine) was bought at the time by Ald. H. F. Wilkins, or on his behalf, and set up in his garden at The Mount, to the west of the town.

It was bequeathed to the town by his grand-daughter, Miss E. F. Wilkins, who died at The Mount last March.

The Borough Council decided that the column should be put up as near as possible to the site of the market, which the Town Hall covers, and research by the Borough Surveyor, Mr. W. T. Jones, has shown the spot in which it has been placed.

It has been mounted on a stone base removed from another part of the town, which is believed to have formed part of the Buttercross, though it may not have carried the particular column that rests on it now.

A sub-committee of the Borough Housing Committee is preparing the wording for a plaque, which will be fixed on the column.

Market Hall pillar returned near to its original location

Two cottages in West End were also sold to James Fisher for £145. Any commons rights derived from the 1770 Enclosure were not included in the sale.

CHIPPING NORTON, November 18 1842.

Cr. The Town Hall Building Committee

(One hundred & six pounds (Jas Fisher Purchase)

in Account with

I & C D. Matthews.

£106 " "

John Matthews

CHIPPING NORTON, Feby 10 1843.

Cr. The Market Hall Committee

by James Dawling Esqr Twenty five pounds

in Account with

I & C D. Matthews.

£25 " "

John Matthews

Two banking slips dated 1842 and 1843 connected with the building of the Town Hall.

A copy of the original account is shown overleaf

		Paid on acct	Balances	
Meades & Co	1011-7-6	910 —	101-7-6	
Gearing	326-12-2	200	126-12-2	
Mathews	176-2-9	145	31-2-9	
Herbert	121-9-4	90	31-9-4	
Hewett	171-7-0	120,	51-7-0	
Labour	22-16-8	22-16-8		
Bayliss & [illegible] for [illegible]	7-6-2	7-6-2		
Cartage	1-5-0	1-5-0		
Gratton	23-8-6	23-8-6		
Mr Lee Iron work &c	136-10-6	136-10-6		
Baruch	1-10-6	1-10-6		
Smith	8-1-6	8-1-6		
Mr Aplin	35-18-1	35-18-1		
Gas Company	1-2-3	1-2-3		
[illegible] [illegible] & Co [illegible] Slater	70-7-5	70-7-5		
Clearing [illegible]	7-0-0		7-0-0	
	2122-5-2	1773-6-5	348-18-9	
Work to Gas House	2-14-10	348-18-9	2-14-10	
	2125-0-0	2122-5-2	351-13-7	
Mr Lee Account not [illegible]				
Received in Subscriptions				626-10-0
— By Old Market Town Hall Cottages & Waste Lands				663-8-6
Elm Tree				9 —
Advanced by J H Langston Esqr				500
				1798-[illegible]
Deficiency				326-[illegible]
				£2125-0-[illegible]
[illegible] Subscriptions made [illegible]	4[illegible]			

CHIPPING-NORTON.

TO BE SOLD BY AUCTION,

BY DAVID MALLETT,

At the Town Hall in Chipping-Norton, on Tuesday the 8th of March, 1842, at 6 o'clock in the evening,

(UNDER CONDITIONS THEN TO BE PRODUCED)

With the approbation of the Lords Commissioners of her Majesty's Treasury

THE UNDERMENTIONED LOTS OF

FREEHOLD PROPERTY,

Situate in the Borough of Chipping-Norton, belonging to the Corporation:

LOT 1.

A BUILDING

SITUATE IN GODDARD'S LANE, CALLED THE

TOWN HALL,

Consisting of one large Room above, and two rooms underneath, used as a Prison and Engine House.

LOT 2.

Three Cottages,

Situate in the West End of the town, in the respective occupations of Joseph Groves, George Webb, and Thomas Goodway; having Gardens detached, *with a Right of Pasturage* on the Chipping-Norton Commons, in respect of the cottage now occupied by the said Joseph Groves.

This Lot will be sold subject to a Road through the passage from the street, and the use of the Well, for the benefit of the purchaser of Lot 3.

LOT 3.

A Piece of Garden Ground

Behind Lot 2, well stocked with fruit trees, in the occupation of Mr. Fisher, containing by admeasurement 34 Perches.

Lots 2 and 3 will be sold subject to any supposed out-going, chargeable upon or payable out of the same.

Further particulars may be obtained on application at the office of Mr. WESTON APLIN, the Town Clerk of Chipping-Norton.

SMITH, PRINTER, CHIPPING-NORTON.

Accounts in the Minute Book dated 19th August 1842 show entries of some of the sales:

	£	s	d
Mr Hieatt	25	0	0
Henry Tilsley	14	13	9
John Matthews	61	10	0
John Matthews	5	0	0
Mr Ward	119	0	0
John Hood	5	0	0
	230	3	9

The new Town Hall was built on arches, and the entrance to the Main Hall was, as now, on the eastern side up the flight of steps through the large pillars.
The Council chamber was also on this floor.

In addition to the new Town Hall, the council decided to install a "Weighing Machine" underneath the building to collect tolls, and include a space for the fire engine.
Mr Weston Aplin (the Town Clerk, who was also an attorney) offered to loan £100 to purchase the machine.
The company Bradley & Co. were successful in acquiring the contract and an order for a *"machine of the best construction"* was placed with them.
A committee of the Council was set up to proceed with the erection of the machine and authorised to spend up to £100.

At a meeting on 11th August 1843, it was reported that authority had been received from Her Majesty's Treasury to mortgage a toll house and the weighing machine as a security for Mr Aplin.

William Hood was appointed as Superintendent of the machine for six months and to receive one third of the tolls as remuneration for his services.

Until direct communication with the coalfield was established by the opening of the railway, the weighbridge played an important part in the household economy of the town. Before this time all coal was brought from Banbury by cart and weighed before delivery to purchasers.

At the Council meeting held on 13th October 1843, it was reported that it would be necessary to repair a considerable number of broken windows in the Town Hall.

These had been caused by a violent freak hailstorm on 9th August which had also inflicted severe damage to crops and broken windows in practically every house in the town. A subscription list for the district had been opened, headed by Queen Victoria who gave £100 and Prince Albert £50.

The total loss for the town was £2,656.5s.4d, and this was paid out to 219 claimants, including 87 allotment holders.

At their meeting held on 9th November 1843, it was resolved that William Hood should pay over the tolls to the Borough Treasurer (John Liddiard) quarterly in November, February, May and August.

On 14th February 1845 it was resolved to sell two of the common stints, held over at the time of the sale of land for £12 each to provide railings for outside the Town Hall. These stints were purchased by Messrs Weston Aplin and John Matthews and were later conveyed to them on 8th August 1845.

On 4th February 1847, the Council agreed that the magistrates could use the Town Hall for "Petty Sessions" and other business connected with their office.

In 1849, the illuminated clock with bell-turret was added to the north end of the building, paid for by public subscription, the money raised being £170.18s.6d.

The Banbury Guardian, 15th March 1849

"Within the last fortnight a turret in the form of an arch, corresponding in design with other parts of the building, has been erected on the north front of the Town Hall, and in which the bell, on which the clock will strike, was erected on Monday last, and which weighs over 3 cwt."

The Banbury Guardian, 3rd May 1849

"Town Hall clock completed, pendulum seven feet long – a beautiful specimen of a simple but ingenious contrivance by which the clock turns the gas full on, or reduces it to the size of a pea, at the appointed minute. Dial 3½ feet in diameter. Made by Mr. Simms."

(The gas light illuminated the clock face at night.)

At a later date the weather vane, in the form of a foxhound, was added, given by members of the Heythrop Hunt.

A list showing the individual subscribers and the amounts given is shown on page 13.

CHIPPING-NORTON.

LIST OF SUBSCRIBERS FOR A TOWN CLOCK.

	£	s.	d.
Aplin, Weston	2	2	0
Anstice, Captain G. ..	1	0	0
Allen, William, *Baker*		1	0
Allen, William		1	0
Aries, William		2	6
Artiss, William		1	0
Andrews, Richard		1	0
Akerman, William ..		1	0
Aldsworth, William ..		2	6
Barter, Rev C.	2	0	0
Brooks, Rev. J. H. ..	1	1	0
Beck, Rev. James....		10	0
Bliss, Rev. T.	1	1	0
Baker, Rev. W.		2	6
Bliss, William	5	5	0
Bishop, William	1	1	0
Bowen, Benj.	1	1	0
Belcher, Henry	1	1	0
Bankes, John S.	[illegible]	0	0
Beck, John		10	0
Biggerstaff, John		10	0
Beechey, John		5	0
Bowles, William ..		2	6
Bartlett, George		2	6
Bartlett, James		2	6
Boscott, John		2	6
Barnes, Mary Ann ..		1	0
Buswell, William.. ..		5	0
Budge, John		5	0
Bettridge, James ..		2	6
Berrill, James		1	0
Brooks, John		1	0
Bowles, John		2	6
Burden, Charles		2	6
Berry, John		1	0
Bowles, Mary Ann ..		1	0
Bowles, Sarah		1	0
Butler, James		1	0
Blackwell, William ..		1	0
Bishop, Thomas			6
Colvile, Capt. F.	[illegible]	0	0
Coldicott, William ..	[illegible]	0	0
Conquer, Henry		1	0
Cumberbatch, L. T. ..		10	6
Chafy, W. W.		10	0
Cook, Richard		2	6
Clifton, John		1	0
Coleman, Mary......			6
Coles, William		1	0
Claridge, Benjamin .		2	6
Cack, Mary Ann			3
Cross, Joseph			6
Dawkins Colonel	5	0	0
Draper, John, *Baker* .	1	1	0
Dodd, Edward ..		10	0
Draper, George		5	0
Dunford, William ...		2	6
Dring, Nath.		2	6
Dooley, Hannah		1	0
Day, Ann			6
Dipple, William		1	0
Dunning, Thomas....			6
Eldridge, Rev. R.	2	2	0
Edwards, William		5	0
Endall, James		5	0
Eggleston, Ann		2	6
Endall, Richard ..		2	6
Eaton, John		1	0
Edgar, William		1	0
Eaton, William		1	0
Eaton, Thomas		1	0
Endall, Elizabeth ..			3
Farwell, John	2	2	0
Ford, E. D.	2	2	0
Fisher, James	1	1	0
Carried up......£37	37	15	6

	£	s.	d.
Brought up	37	15	6
Friends, Five		5	0
Friends, Seven		7	0
Faulkner, Joseph			6
Ford, William		1	0
Franklin, F.		1	0
Gardner, George	1	0	0
Gordon, I. R. ..	1	0	0
Guy, Samuel	1	1	0
Gibbs, John	1	1	0
Greenwood, Henry ..	1	1	0
Gardner, Henry	1	1	0
Gulliver, Thomas	1	1	0
Gearing, William ...		10	0
Golby, Thomas		5	0
Gardner, William		2	6
Galpin, Robert ..		5	0
Gardner, Thomas ..		2	6
Gostley, Thomas		5	0
Gamble, William		2	6
Gibbs, James		2	6
Giles, William ..		2	6
Gibbs, Richard . ..		1	0
Gibbs, Joseph . .		1	0
Gee, Charles		1	0
Gillam, H. J.		2	6
Gee, Daniel		5	0
Green, James			6
Gee, Isaac		1	0
Grant, William			6
Groves, James		1	0
Green, William		1	0
Green, Charles		1	0
Hitchman, W. S.	5	5	0
Hitchman, Miss . .	1	1	0
Hitchman John		10	0
Hellier, Rev. T. S. ..	1	1	0
Hopgood, Thomas ..	2	2	0
Hall, Tawney and Co.	2	0	0
Hammersley, H. M.	1	1	0
Holmes, Charles	1	1	0
Hartley, E. K.	1	1	0
Hartley, Edward ..	1	1	0
Hieatt, John	1	1	0
Hood, John	1	1	0
Hodgkins and Son ..	1	1	0
Holloway, Misses....		10	6
Huckvale, William ..		10	0
Harris, George		10	0
Hunt, Timms		7	6
Herbert, Thomas		5	0
Hood, Edward ...		5	0
Hodgkins, Dan ..		2	0
Hopkins, Edward ...		2	6
Herbert, William		1	0
Hathaway, John ..		1	0
Holtham, Thos. ...		1	0
Hall, William		1	0
Herbert, Charles ..		2	6
Hall, Charles		1	0
Hall, E.		1	0
Haynes, Mary		2	6
Hood and Gardner ..		5	0
Hathaway, George ..		2	6
Hieatt, Nehemiah ...		1	0
Haynes, Richard		1	0
Hawkins, William ..		1	0
Hall, William			6
Hall, Henry			6
Hall, Thomas			6
Hooper, William			6
Hautin Joseph			6
Hathaway, R. P. ..		10	6
Ivings, William		10	0
Insall, William			6
Insall, George			6
Carried up......£72	72	12	0

	£	s.	d.
Brought up	72	12	0
James, R. S.		10	6
Jennings, Edward . .		10	0
Joines, Job		1	0
Jennings, Edw., Jun. .		2	6
Jones, John		1	0
Jones, Robert		1	0
Johnson, Felix		2	6
Kingdon, I. H.	2	2	0
Keck, Thomas	1	1	0
Keck, E. H.		10	6
Keck, Elizabeth .		10	0
Kirtland, James		10	0
Keitley, John		5	0
Kirtland, David		1	0
Kirtland, William ..		1	0
Kearsey, Richard ...		2	0
Langston, J. H., M.P.	5	0	0
Lockwood, Rev. J. W.		10	0
Loveland, Jacob	1	1	0
Luckett, William ..		10	0
Liddiard, John		5	0
Luckett, James		2	6
Lusty, Aaron			6
Law, Urban		1	0
Laskey, John		2	6
Lord, John		1	0
Mitchell, Rev. John	1	1	0
Malins, George	1	0	0
Mathews, J., *Painter*		10	6
Malins, Joseph		10	6
Matthews, George ..		10	6
Mace, Thomas		5	0
Margetts, Richard ..		7	6
Meace, Henry		2	6
Moods, Richard		2	6
Matthews, Robert....		2	6
Malins, John		2	0
Makepeace, John		2	6
Malins, W. S.		2	6
Malins, J. F.		1	0
Malins, George		1	0
Mace, John		2	6
Matthews, Richard ..		2	6
Moore, Joseph			6
Matthews, J., *Weaver*		1	0
Matthews, Jane ..			6
Moss, John		1	0
Margetts, John		1	0
Mason, Daniel		1	0
Moss, Hannah			3
Nason, William		1	0
Nason, Thomas			6
Nason, Maria			3
Nurden, Charlotte ..			3
Nason, Elizabeth ..			3
Philips, Sir George ..	3	0	0
Penyston, Miss	1	1	0
Parsons, Robert	5	5	0
Peel, William	1	0	0
Pettipher, Thomas ..	1	1	0
Phipps and Son	1	1	0
Palmer, Samuel	1	1	0
Potter, Misses		10	6
Phillips, Thomas		10	6
Pryer, Samuel		10	6
Phillips, Richard		10	0
Phillips, Mrs.		10	0
Phillips, John		5	0
Porter, Richard		2	6
Carried up ...£108	108	18	6

	£	s.	d.
Brought up	108	18	6
Paine, George		1	0
Padley, John		2	0
Palmer, Richard		2	0
Packer, Charles		2	6
Pease, George			6
Padley, Timothy ..		2	0
Phillips, John ...		1	0
Porter, Charles ...		1	0
Quy, J. M.	1	1	0
Quatermaine, Joseph..		10	0
Redesdale, Rt. Hon. Ld.	2	0	0
Rawlinson, A. L. ..	3	3	0
Rolls, Thomas	3	3	0
Ryland, Emma		2	6
Ryland, Elizabeth ..		2	6
Robinson, Thomas ..		2	6
Randell, John		2	0
Stevens, Rev. W. E...	1	1	0
Sotham, Frederick ..	1	1	0
Simms and Son	2	2	0
Stephan, J. H.		10	6
Smith, G. M.	1	1	0
Salter, W. H.		5	0
Stanbridge, Catherine .		5	0
Symonds, Susan		2	6
Spence, William ...		2	6
Smith, Stephen		5	0
Summerton, Peter ..		5	0
Smith, John		2	0
Simms, Thomas ...		5	0
Simms, Frederick		5	0
Scarsbrook, Edward ..		1	0
Spain, Henry		5	0
Scarsbrook, Edward .		2	0
Scarsbrook, William .		1	0
Stevens, James		1	0
Smith, Thomas ...			6
Scarsbrook, Ann ..			6
Scarsbrook, Jane ..			6
Tilsley, George F.....	2	2	0
Tilsley, Henry	1	1	0
Timms, George		10	0
Trafford, Henry ..		5	0
Timms, Elizabeth ..		2	6
Townsend, Thomas .		1	0
Trafford, William ..		2	6
Tate, James		1	0
Townsend, Sophia ..			3
Trinder, John ...		1	0
Tranter, James ...			6
Teasle, Simeon ..			6
Wilkins, H. F.	2	2	0
Woodhouse, W. H. .	2	2	0
Wootten, Richard ..	2	2	0
Whippy, B. J. ...	1	0	0
Ward, John	1	0	0
Wells, Francis	1	1	0
Wilson, Ernest		10	0
Williams, Thomas ..		5	0
Wilks, William		2	6
Whitehouse, C. F. ..		5	0
Williams, Robert ..		1	0
Ward, Sophia		1	0
Wheeler, Edward		1	0
Williams, Samuel ..		5	0
Walker, Elizabeth ..			3
Webb, George			6
Yeates, Charles		2	6
TOTAL £143	143	7	0

G. M. SMITH, PRINTER, CHIPPING-NORTON.

Additional Subscriptions } 27.11.6

170.18.6

[signature]
24th May 1869

It was not long before the Overseers of the Poor would be asked to hand over money from the Poor Relief Fund, anything from £50 to £100 per annum (paid half yearly) to help the Borough Fund and by 1851 this had risen to £140 a year.

Another suggestion put forward was that the Town Hall should be let out for Public Auctions at not less than a guinea (£1.1s.0d in pre-decimal money) a day plus the expense of cleaning the room afterwards.

On 23rd December 1851 the Mayor Cllr George Tilsley reported that he had been asked in a letter from Mr JH Langston MP if the Council would consider putting in three cells underneath the Town Hall to secure prisoners awaiting committal to Oxford prison.

The cost of doing this would be £40 and the Quarter Sessions at Oxford had agreed to pay £5 a year.

This was then put into being and by 9th November 1852 the rental was increased to £10 a year to be paid on "*Lady Day*[*]".

---

[*] ***(Lady Day, the name given to 25th March, in the Christian Calendar it is the day of the annunciation of the Virgin Mary and is a quarter day in England and Ireland)***

On 1st March 1853, a letter was received from the Clerk of the Peace, Mr William Davenport written to the Clerk for the Petty Sessions, Mr Rawlinson of the Chadlington and Banbury South Division.

It requested that a twenty-five year lease be granted for the cells and a room for the Constable at £15 pa, and that when not required by them the Council could use any unoccupied cells. They would furnish the cells and room and repair any wilful damage caused by prisoners.
The Council would be asked to provide a servant of the Constable at all times to aid in the custody of the prisoners in the cells.

At a meeting held on 8th August 1862 the Council gave their permission for a new Police Station to be built on Victoria Gardens, a triangle of land between London Road, Banbury Road Crossing (once known as "Treacle Lane") and Banbury Road. The gardens had been laid out in 1840 to commemorate the royal wedding between Victoria and Albert. This prompted a series of discussions between the Council and the Justices as to what was to happen to the agreement to rent the cells under the town hall, once the new Police Station was in use.

By May 1866 the Council had finally agreed to accept £60, by way of releasing the County Council from the lease. In addition, the Justices were to have free use of the cells at the police station for Borough prisoners.

Following this change, the Council decided to re-vamp the lower floor of the Town Hall to provide a reading room (to be let to the Literary Institute), a courtroom, and a room plus facilities for a Judge.

Since an estimate of £300 was required to provide these changes, permission was sought from the Treasury and this was forthcoming by May 1867. The contractor agreed to provide a kitchen range or hotplate, and a boiler for an additional £10 plus gas for light and water pipes for the closets for a further £10. The cost for a year's supply of water was £3.10s.0d.

A copy of the original estimate which was submitted in detail on A3 size paper is on the following pages.

Details of Estimate for the proposed Alterations to the Town Hall Chipping Norton

Reading Room and Market Hall

Take down & carry away old cells	3 .. 10 .. 0
10¼ Sqr 1¼ Yel Floor & Joists 4½ x 3 60/- a laid on oak sleepers for the old bricks	30 .. 15 .. 0
6 pair 2 sashes & frames with semi heads Chord bar lines, weights Oak sills, glazed with 2nds 21 oz sheet 7 x 5 each 2/3 80/-	24 .. 0 .. 0
6 Iron air bricks	.. 6 .. 0
186 Yds plast^g 3 coat good Work 9^d	6 .. 19 .. 6
6 stone sills 6 9 x 4 & fix^g 2/-	3 .. 12 .. 0
1 pr 2¼ fold^g doors cir^r fan light strong frame 10 x 5 & fast^gs	5 .. 10 .. 0
120 ft skirting 4^d	2 .. 0 .. 0
dig out foundations for and wall up under windows 5 ft wide with free stone plinth to match old	5 .. 0 .. 0
6 Window boards and bearers 5/-	1 .. 10 .. 0
Cutting out and trim^g for stair case	1 .. 0 .. 0
New stair case 4 .. 6 wide and 14 ft high with hand and ballusters	11 .. 7 .. 6
Construct fire place from Basement with register chimney piece complete	20 .. 0 .. 0
154 Yds 9 brick work 6/-	46 .. 4 .. 0
18 9 x 4 Lintols 7½ 9 x 6 D^o	1 .. 0 .. 0
2 Water closets with pan Appar^t comp	10 .. 0 .. 0
1 . 2 Door & Jambs 3 . 1½ Ditto molding & fastg^s	6 .. 0 .. 0
1 frame ledged door 42 ft & strong frame & fastg^s	3 .. 0 .. 0
Forw^d	181 .. 14 .. 0

Brot Forward 181 . 14 . 0

To borrowed lights to Water Closets 1 . 0 . 0

Wall up one doorway into cell and form new opening with door and frame } 2 . 0 . 0

Lintol to support beam in absence of pillar — . 16 . 0

Take up old brick floor make up the ground 6 or 8 inches and relay 76 yards brick flat in Market Hall passages & Water Closets 1/3 } 4 . 15 . 0

36 pr 5 drain pipes digging out for & setting to Water Closets 9d } 1 . 7 . 0

Pull out old opening and make good to the weighing Machine } 1 . 0 . 0

1 Door & frame to Ditto fix old desk 1 . 5 . 0

Remove & refix present Iron gates . 15 . 0

2 solid stones in door ways 12 x 4 1 . 0 . 0

Market Hall 1 window & 1 sill as before 4 . 12 . 0

53 yds plastering to Water Closets only 8d 1 . 15 . 0

Whitening ceilings coloring walls of the passages and Market Room only } 2 . 0 . 0

Cistern to hold 150 gallons with 40 pr 3/4 Iron pipes bends &c from the main Hall tap & waste } 7 . 10 . 0

Painting in 3 oils and 4 Oils outside } 10 . 10 . 0

Agreed for the extention of the Area and railing } 10 . 0 . 0

Forward 231 . 18 . 0

	Brot Forward	231 . 18 . 0
Judges Room		
	4 3/4 square Floor & Joists as before 60/	12 . 15 . 0
	Add on this Floor for about 8 yds of Maws tiling 5/	2 . 0 . 0
	New 2 door cir^r fan light as before (about 60 feet) with frame & fast^s	3 . 0 . 0
	3 Air bricks	– . 3 . 0
	Water Closet complete (mahog ?)	5 . 0 . 0
	Stair case to Council Chamber with hand rails ballusters complete	11 . 11 . 0
	Triming & making good	1 . 0 . 0
	4 Doors Jambs moldings & fast^g mold^d one side	6 . 0 . 0
	53 Yds ½ brick petitions & foundations 3/6	9 . 5 . 6
	4 Window sills as before	2 . 8 . 0
	4 Window beams & boards	1 . 0 . 0
	4 Windows as before	11 . 0 . 0
	Repair ceilings	1 . 0 . 0
	200 Yds 3 coat plaster Walls & petitions 9^d	7 . 10 . 0
	Chimney piece & register forming fireplace	10 . 0 . 0
	130 feet skirting 6	3 . 5 . 0
	Wash hand bason & water laid on	1 . 10 . 0
	Painting as before	5 . 10 . 0
		332 . 15 . 6

Allowed for old materials

Old doors	5 . 0 . 0
Bricks	5 . 0 . 0
Stone Work	5 . 0 . 0
Iron Railings	10 . 0 . 0
	25 . 0 . 0

	25 . 0 . 0
	£ 307 . 15 . 6

By November 1867 terms were submitted to the Literary Institute for the Reading Room as follows:

1. That the Institute should pay for the whole gas passing through the meter and that 2/6d be repaid to them by the Council for every occasion on which the Town Hall may be publicly used for gas light.
2. A yearly rent of £3.0s.0d be paid half-yearly.
3. The Institute to pay £2.10s.0d for water closets for the first year and succeeding years such sum as the Council may fix.
4. That the room be given up clean on all such occasions as the Council may require.
5. The Institute to provide a Fire Guard.
6. A person shall be in attendance during such time as the room is open and who shall effectively close the room at night and extinguish the fire and gas.
7. All damage that may be done be made good by the Institute.
8. The Council to have the option of determining the use of the room by the Institute on giving three months' notice at any time of the year.

Finally, after a further meeting with the Institute, the Council agreed to 3/6d per occasion instead of 2/6d. Also, because the Institute said they had very little available funds, the Council agreed that no rent need be paid in the first year.

In 1872 the town became an Urban Sanitary Authority with increased powers and responsibility for improving sewerage and public health. Monthly meetings were introduced. In addition, several committees were formed to cope with the increasing work.

By 1878 a new fire engine was purchased and a new engine house was built in which to keep it. Alterations were made to the bell in the clock tower to be used as a fire-warning bell.

In 1879 it became necessary to make repairs to the chimney and flues in the Town Hall at a cost of £4.18s.0d.

On 29th November 1889 the Council decided that a gallery would be erected at a cost of £400, the money to be raised by a loan to be paid off at the rate of £100 a year for four years. The gallery would include new seating.

It was then decided in 1890 that in future all gas used would be paid for by the Council, and in lieu of this change to the agreement with the Literary Institute, all seats in the Reading Room would become the property of the Council. An entry in the minutes of August 1893 shows that the Town Clerk was instructed to carry out a check of furniture belonging to the Corporation.

2 deal top tables
14 oak chairs
87 cane seat chairs
11 old seats
12 new seats in the gallery
Oak table
2 oak elbow chairs
20 new seats
8 long forms

In the same year, a specialist was called in to examine and report on the deterioration of the portrait of Alderman HF Wilkins.

The expert, a Mr Harper of Criceth, concluded that the damage was mainly caused by greasy vapour combined with cold conditions and that the caretaker should be *"called to account"*.

However, when he had cleaned and applied several coats of heavy varnish to the painting, there was no permanent damage.

He also mentioned that the frame was in good order and that the gilding was good for at least five years. To my knowledge, the frame has not been re-gilded to this day!

D2

Borough of  Chipping Norton.

SCALE OF CHARGES

FOR THE USE OF

The Town Hall and Ante-rooms.

	To Residents in the Borough. £	s.	d.	To Non-Residents £	s.	d.
1—For an Ordinary Meeting in the Hall during Daytime		5	0		7	6
2—For Hall, for an Evening Meeting, with Gas and Fire		7	6		10	6
3—The Hall for a Day and (including Gas and Fire) for the Evening		12	0		18	0
4—The Council Chamber or Committee Room during Daytime and without Gas or Fire ...		1	6		2	6
5—For an ordinary Evening Meeting in either of these Rooms, with Gas and Fire		3	0		5	0
6—Council Chamber or Committee Room for a Day, and (with Gas and Fire) for the Evening		4	0		6	6
7—For the Smoke Room for a Meeting during Daytime or Evening		1	6		2	0
8—The Hall and above Ante-rooms for a Day and (inclusive of Gas and Fires) for the Evening		15	0	1	10	0
9—For each following Day and Evening ...		12	6	1	5	0
10—The Hall and above Ante-rooms for a Day and Night, including Gas and Fires ...	1	5	0	—	—	—
11—For the use of the Reading Room (36 hours' notice to be given in all cases by persons desiring the use of the Reading Room) ...		5	0		7	6

The above Charges to include the Hall-keeper's Services.

The leave of the Mayor to be first obtained, who may decide any case or application not implied in the above particulars, and the Charges to be paid to the Town Clerk BEFORE using the Hall or Rooms, and only on the date and time paid for as specified on receipt.

THOMAS MACE, Town Clerk.

10th July, 1903.

HAYES, TYP.

In 1908 the Chipping Norton Light and Power Company started laying electricity supplies throughout the town and the Town Hall changed over from gas.

The start of the Great War in 1914 saw the Town Hall being used extensively for fundraising concerts—there are many references in the minutes of the Council.

ENGLAND DECLARES WAR ON GERMANY No 4
CROWD WATCHING THE CHIPPING NORTON TERRITORIAL'S GOING ON SERVICE AUG 5TH 1914

November 1914: free use of the hall for a Sacred Concert with proceeds to the Belgian Relief Fund, and for a concert of the Choral Society with proceeds going to the Red Cross Local Working Party.

December 1914: free use of the hall for a Christmas Party for wives and children of soldiers and sailors serving in the war and for Belgian refugees.

The minutes of December 1914 also record the appointment of a new caretaker, Miss Edith Hall, on a salary of 10/6d a week, to start on 1st January 1915.

February 1915: free use of the hall for the National Children's Home concert in aid of Queen Mary's Work for Women Fund, and for a Charlbury Patriotic Society concert with proceeds going to help Belgian refugees.

April 1915: free use of the hall by the Oddfellow's for three nights a month when their hall is in use as a hospital, and permission to use the Hall by the Picture Palace if they also have to move.
There was also a request by Oxfordshire County Council for their Cooking Classes and this was agreed on the basis that any profits went to The Prince of Wales Relief fund.

May 1915: free use of the hall for a Smoking Concert in aid of the Belgian Relief fund.
The Town Hall continued to be used to support the war effort until the Armistice was declared.

The photograph on page 26 shows the Mayor, Mr W Toy, reading the King's proclamation from the Town Hall steps.

CHIPPING NORTON PEACE THANKSGIVING
SUNDAY JULY 6. 1919.
HIS WORSHIP THE MAYOR (WILLIAM TOY ESQR)
READING THE KINGS PROCLAMATION

THE TABLES READY FOR THE SUPPER GIVEN BY HIS WORSHIP THE MAYOR
W. TOY. ESQR TO THE RETURNED SOLDIERS AND SAILORS
OF CHIPPING

Following the Great War and the return of service personnel to the town, the Town Hall returned to its former role as a venue for many varied functions, though times were very hard. As elsewhere in the country, the town had paid a high price in the loss of lives.

The main concerns of the Borough Council was to concentrate on the provision of housing, better public health, water quality and the things which in peacetime make for a good community. This was to continue throughout the twenties and thirties, until once again a World War broke out in 1939.

The Council minute books again reveal the central role the Town Hall played in the conflict.

9th November 1939

6th Battalion of the Durham Light Infantry given permission to use the Town Hall kitchen as a Troops canteen, subject to the same not being handed over to the NAAFI or sub-let; terms were agreed for cleaning.
It was also agreed that Chaplains could use the Hall for Sunday Services for soldiers billeted in the town.

13th September 1940

The Council agreed for use to be made of the Town Hall kitchen and Reading Room to provide mid-day meals for refugees residing in the Borough

11th October 1940
Councillors Freeman, Gibbs, Hall, Marshall, Smith and Warmington elected to form the "Spitfire Fund Committee".

Council agreed to use of the Hall for the Badminton Club.

9th November 1940
Council agreed to the use of the Reading Room and adjoining cloakroom as an Infant Welfare Centre, and for a short period troops were billeted at the town hall.

13th June 1941
Council agreed to a loan of £50 to be made available to the Garden Fruit Committee to enable them to make payments, pending the receipt of the proceeds of a sale of jam, and that they could use a room and kitchen when available.

8th August 1941
Part time use of the Town Hall by one of the Defence Services granted, subject to rental and other services being agreed. Council agreed to use of the Town Hall for War Weapons Week.

10th October 1941
Permission given for the Home Guard to fix a notice board to the Town Hall.

10th November 1941

Oxfordshire Education Committee to be informed that the Council are prepared to let them use the kitchen and Reading Room for feeding school children until the British Restaurant is opened, the rent to be 10/- per week plus 2/- for electricity, and that they supply their own fuel for cooking and pay for a cleaner.

28th November 1941

The Fire Force Commander was asked to provide a "Static Tank" holding 10,000 gallons of water in the town centre for emergency fire fighting.

18th February 1942

Council agreed use of the Hall for "Warships Week".

Fur and Feather Club allowed to use the Reading Room on 7th March on usual terms, subject to the room being vacated by 6.30pm and cleaned and disinfected immediately thereafter.

13th March 1942

It was proposed that, until the cessation of hostilities, for all future bookings of the Town Hall for dances a condition be introduced that they should cease at 11.30pm (this was changed in 1943 to 12.30, subject to agreement with the police).

Permission given to the Warships Week Committee to erect an indicator board and platform and saluting base on the Market Square and to lose the Market Square when required during Warships Week.

11th May 1942

Council recommend half charges to be made to Civil Defence Services when using the hall for lectures, and the same to apply to lectures by Oxfordshire Special Constabulary.

Free use of the Town Hall for the Hospital Carnival Committee on 4th July.

Permission given for the Welfare Clinic to use the large hall instead of the Reading Room.

11th September 1942
Council decide they should not agree to let the Town Hall for any political meetings on Sundays.

8th January 1943
An application was received from a military unit to book the Town Hall every two or three weeks for Dances and Whist Drives; the Council resolved that only one booking at a time could be accepted.

12th February 1943
Army Blood Transfusion Service granted use of the Town Hall on 21st February 1943.

12th March 1943
Free use of the Town Hall granted for a concert given by the County Regiment during Army Week.

At a meeting held on 11th May 1945 the Mayor proposed that a loyal message be sent to His Majesty the King on the occasion of the victorious end of hostilities in Europe.

And so through yet another long and costly World War the Town Hall played a major part in supporting the war effort.

Extensive celebrations were to follow shortly afterwards, and again in August 1945, with the defeat of Japan.

On 3rd March 1950 the Town Hall was seriously damaged by a fire which started in the lower part of the building. The local fire brigade was called at 4.18am by Miss Mary Sirl, the Manageress of The Corner Café who lived above the shop.

Other Fire Brigades from around the County also attended but the fire took hold rapidly.

Fortunately the Town's Mace, Mayor's robes, Mayor's chair and other furniture, plus Past Mayors' photographs, the large mirror and most of the paintings were saved as were the majority of the books from the Reading Room.

Efforts to save the Town Hall were hampered by scaffolding in the upper hall which was in the process of redecoration, but the fact that the "Static Tank", containing many gallons of water, was still in the town centre made it possible to save the shell of the building. However, the interior, including the roof, was completely destroyed.

The picture below shows the "Static Tank" in the town centre.

The Mayor, Councillor AG Brindle, very quickly launched a public appeal, the books from the Reading Room were transferred to the Friend's Meeting House in New Street, and the Co-operative Society offered the Borough Council the use of their Hall, Board Room and Café.

The photograph below taken in 1952 shows a Council meeting being held in the Co-operative Hall.

Some of the larger items, such as the paintings which had some water damage, were stored by local businesses.

The building was restored by 1952 at a cost of £18,725 of which £8,150 was claimed by way of insurance.
The Mayor's Appeal, apart from the many offers of help, raised £1,670.

Fortunately, we still have paintings and items rescued from the fire, and additional ones which have been acquired since that time.

The following photographs show the extent of the damage.

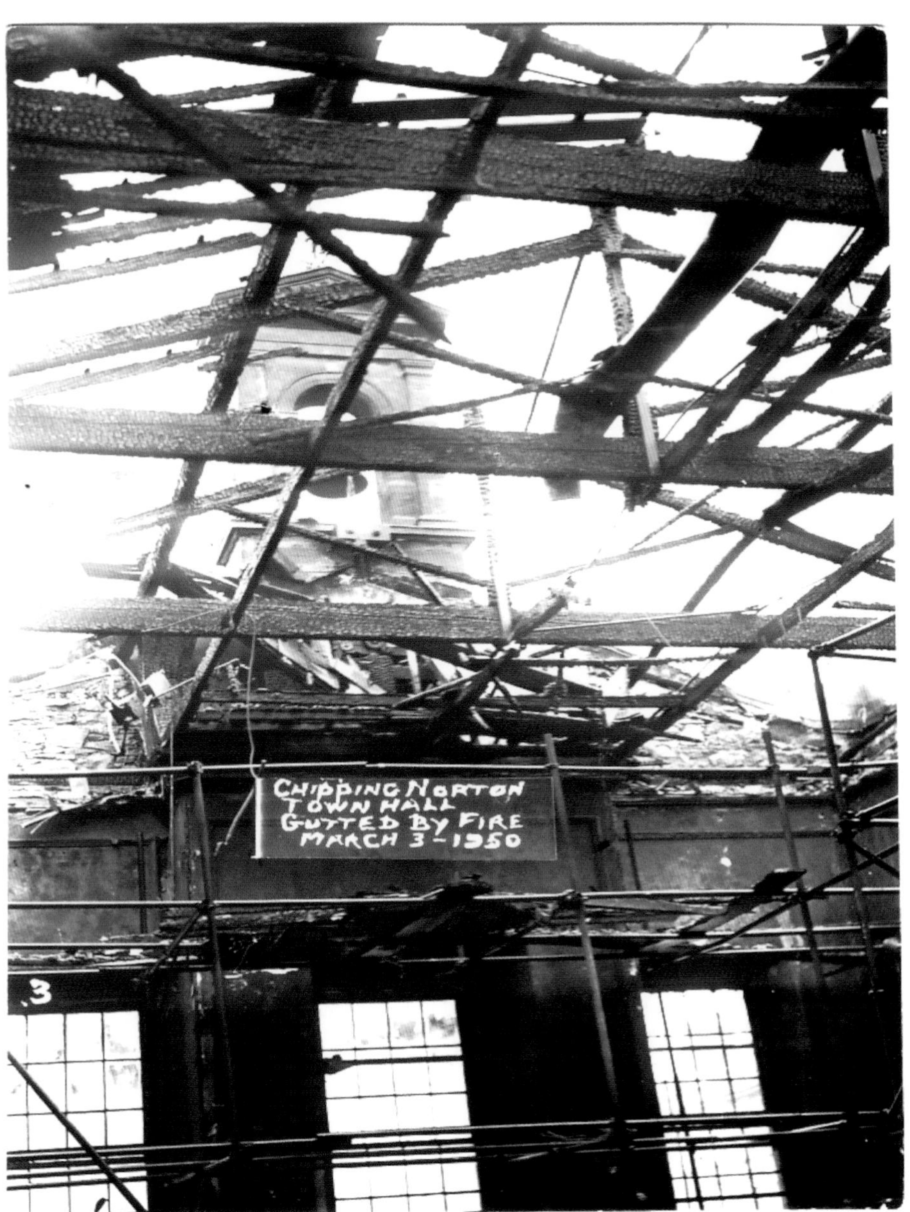
CHIPPING NORTON
TOWN HALL
GUTTED BY FIRE
MARCH 3 - 1950

CHIPPING NORTON
TOWN HALL
DESTROYED BY FIRE
MARCH 3-1950

The photograph overleaf is of the opening of the reconstructed Town Hall on 8th October 1952.

Note: the balcony is at the opposite end of the building, as can be seen by comparing with an earlier photograph (*below*).

OPENING O... THE RECONST...CTED TOWN HALL
BY THE M...YOR COUNCILLOR M... S.A. WEBB J.P.
OCT 8TH 1952

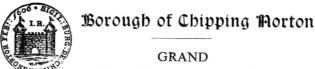

Borough of Chipping Norton

GRAND

Re-Opening Ball

Thursday, October 9th, 1952

8.30 p.m.—1.30 a.m.

Jack Blackman & His Mayfair Orchestra

Evening Dress desirable

DOUBLE 25/-

Dance ticket from the Re-Opening Ball.

In 1960 the external stonework was cleaned and restored at a cost of £5,240 and a grant of £2,940 was received from the Ministry of Works.

In 1974, at the time of the re-organisation of Local Government, the town lost its Borough status and became a Town Council. Most of its responsibilities passed to the newly created West Oxfordshire District Council.

The upper hall of the Town Hall was completely redecorated and new curtains were purchased before the change took place.

Further improvements took place in 1985/6, which included some re-roofing costing £7,500, new lead gutters £6,500, and stonework cleaning £20,000; the kitchen was re-furbished at a cost of £7,923.

In 1989 it was decided to try to solve the problem of disabled access to the upper hall. Alexander Corfield was appointed as Architect for the project and he designed the ramp which now exists, free of charge as his contribution to the scheme.

A committee of the Town Council and representatives of local organisations was formed to establish a joint fund to take the scheme forward.

In the event the contract price was to be £22,372 and it was agreed that the money would be provided in the following way:

Chipping Norton Round Table, Lions and Rotary Clubs would each take up £4,000 interest-free loans for a period of twelve months; Oxfordshire County Council would give a grant of £5,750; and the Town Council would contribute £3,000. There was also a donation of £500 from Country Estates making a total of £21,250. The shortfall would be made up by the Town Council.

A very generous offer was received from Doctors Bruce and Sheila Parker with the following terms: that at the expiry of the twelve-month period of the interest-free loans, they would take over responsibility for outstanding monies and if there was a deficiency in the total of the £12,000, to make this good.

The ramp was built by Messrs Sole Bros., a long-established local firm, which had just been taken over by Kevin Hood and Paul Smith.

A commemorative plaque, now displayed in a cabinet in the Council Chamber, is shown overleaf.

The ramp at the Town Hall was provided in 1991 by contributions from:-

Chipping Norton Lions

Chipping Norton Rotary

Chipping Norton Round Table

Chipping Norton Town Council

Oxfordshire County Council

Country Estates Chipping Norton

H.E.L.P.

Architect

Alexander Corfield RIBA Dip. TP Oxford

Structural Engineer

William B. Hendry BFC C Eng. MICE

Contractor

Sole Bros.

In 2001 problems developed with the striking hammer and bell on the Town Hall clock, and on two occasions these faults had to be rectified – an expensive operation.

The most recent improvements to the lower hall were undertaken in 2003. These involved improvements to toilets and the installation of a baby-changing facility, a room for the Town Hall keeper in the entrance hall (which could also be used as a reception desk to sell tickets at performances), new floors, and a complete upgrading of the Council Chamber and Lower Hall, including a new enlarged and refitted kitchen.

Following the usual tendering process, the contract was awarded to J Townley & Son, a respected local builder, at a cost of £ 96,223.

In 2003, further problems arose with the clock and a specialist company – Smith of Derby – was called in to examine and report. Following their report it was decided to remove broken parts of the clock, including a quarter-horse motor, and convert to a modern T300D self-starting synchronous movement with let-off switch.

The benefit of the new movement, apart from reliability, was that in future any changes for winter/summertime would be automatic. Previously, and for many years, this had to be done manually (along with any other electrical jobs) by Graham Harris – a well-known local electrician.

The photographs show inside the roof of the Town Hall and, at the opposite end in a cupboard, the new workings of the clock.

The motor on the right operates the striking hammer.

Functions held over the years include:

Horticultural shows, amateur dramatic performances, and choir festivals.

Concerts organised by Silver Band, Scouts, Guide's, Women's Institute, Girl's Friendly Society and Choral Societies.

Dinner dances for Mayoral Charities, Royal Antediluvian Order of Buffaloes (Buffs), Masonic, Police, Rotary and Round Table.

Women's Institute and other organisations' cakes and produce sales, coffee mornings to fundraise for local charities and organisations.

Fashion shows, radio and TV broadcasts and wedding receptions.

Old tyme dances, keep-fit demonstrations, local history exhibitions; antique fairs, jumble, book and tool sales, auctions and table-top sales.

Christmas Bazaar's, United Churches and Lawrence Home Nursing Christmas Carol Services; whist drives, bridge club meetings; blood donor sessions and many other local organisations events.

THE CONSERVATIVE SMOKING CONCERT
TOWN HALL CHIPPINGNORTON FEB 15 1912
PACKER'S FLASHLIGHT PHOTO.

THE TEA AND ENTERTAINMENT GIVEN BY THE MAYOR & MAYOR
— COUNCILLOR & MRS J. H. HARTWELL . DEC 30 1920 —

SILVER JUBILEE CELEBRATION
CHIPPING NORTON 1935-64.

CHIPPING NORTON CO-OPERATIVE SOCIETY. 2
STAFF DINNER 1939

CHIPPING NORTON
W.I.
CHRISTMAS PARTY
— 1953 —

1A.

1.

CORONATION TEA
GIVEN BY THE FIRE BRIGADE
CHIPPING NORTON TOWN HALL
— 1953 —

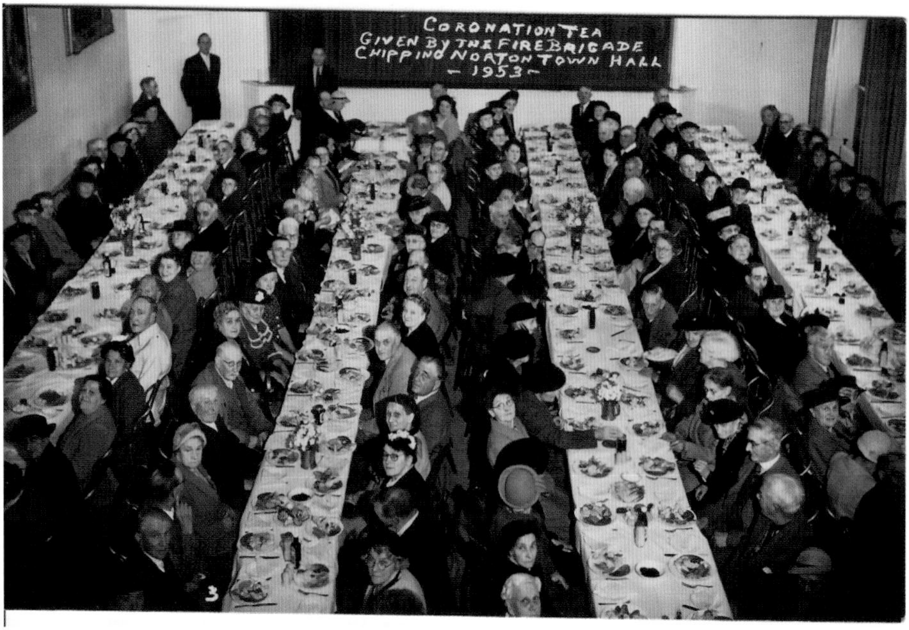

CORONATION TEA
GIVEN BY THE FIRE BRIGADE
CHIPPING NORTON TOWN HALL
- 1953 -
3

CORONATION TEA
GIVEN BY THE FIRE BRIGADE
CHIPPING NORTON TOWN HALL
- 1953 -
5

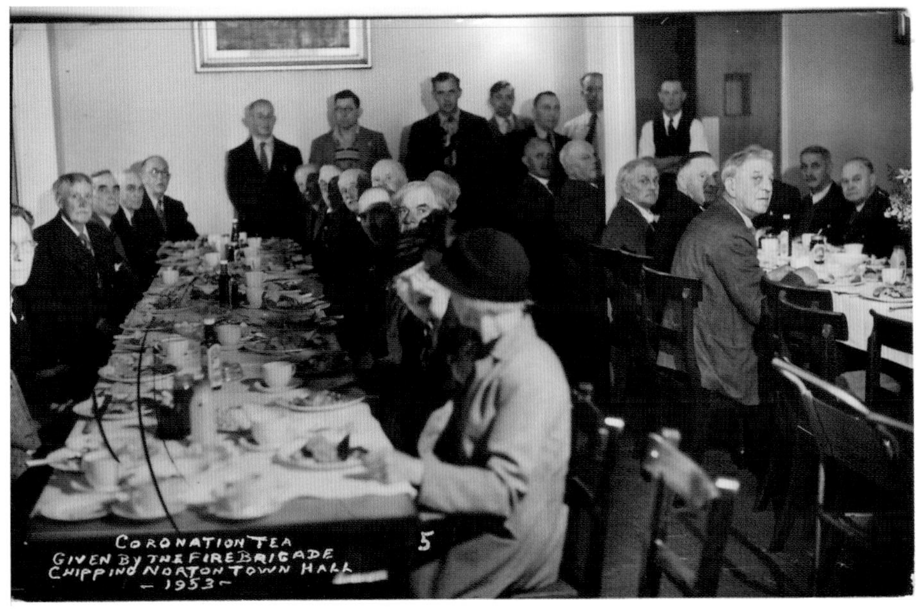

Chipping Norton Horticultural Association show

My wedding reception 17/06/1961 (the band is The Blue Tones)

Fashion show

Dance – Ken Prewers Band

Wilfred Pickles – "Have-a-go"

The Upper Hall, taken from the balcony.

Above the stage in the large hall is the current town seal which denotes the granting of a Charter in the reign of King James I clearly dated Feb 1606.

However, I recently attended a lecture given by Dr Adrienne Rosen **OUDCE*** as part of our 400th year celebrating the granting of our Charter. Dr Rosen revealed that the actual document says "in the fourth year of King James I".

James became King of England in March 1603, and therefore February in the fourth year of his reign would be 1607.

It therefore appears that the year on the seal is incorrect!

*** OUDCE, Oxford University Department of Continuing Education**

The reason for the confusion is that the Gregorian Calendar was adopted in 1752, which changed the start of the New Year from 25th March to 1st January. If the old style calendar had still been in use, the date would have been 1606.

To the right of the stage below the clock is a portrait of Queen Elizabeth II, engraved in mezzotint from a painting by Pietro Annigoni unveiled in 1955.

To celebrate the Queen's 80th birthday, the Radio Times asked its readers to choose the best of ten portraits of the Queen. Annigoni's portrait of the Queen in her garter robes was named the winner.

Information on four paintings in the upper Town Hall, Chipping Norton

On the left is **Alderman Henry Field Wilkins** (Solicitor). He was born in 1804 at Bourton-on-the-Water, Gloucestershire; he came to Chipping Norton in 1833 and went into partnership with George Fawler Tilsley (later to become Wilkins and Toy).

He was Mayor in 1836, 1853, 1861, 1868, 1874, 1876 and 1886, and was the only "Jubilee" Mayor in the country, having filled the office in the year of Queen Victoria's succession and also in the 50th year of her reign.

He lived at The Mount, the grand house built in 1869 on an outcrop of rock adjacent to the Castle Banks.

His son Henry Cromwell Wilkins was also Mayor in 1881 and 1890.

He died in 1891.

On the left of the main entrance is **Albert Brassey, MA, JP, MFH, MP,** who lived at Heythrop House in the late 19th century.

He was born at Rouen, France, in 1844 and was the son of Thomas Brassey, the famous railway contractor who made his fortune building some of the first railways in Britain and abroad.

He was educated at Eton and University College, Oxford, and held a commission in the 14th Hussars.

He became MP for North Oxfordshire and was the High Sheriff of Oxfordshire in 1878.

In 1897 he gave the gold chain to be worn by the Mayor of the Borough to mark the Diamond Jubilee of Queen Victoria, which is still in use today.

He was then chosen as Mayor for the next four years, 1898–1901 and is the only person not a member of the Council to hold the office. It was also the first occasion the office was held by a member of the House of Commons.

He was also Master of Foxhounds of the Heythrop Hunt located on the Worcester Road, so named after his house.

He died in 1918.

On the right of the main entrance is
Matilda Maria Helena (Maude) Brassey, formerly **Bingham**, the wife of Albert Brassey.

She was born in 1851 in Galway, Ireland, and married Albert in 1871. She was the daughter of the 4th Baron Clanmorris. They had eight children, Lily, Rose, May, Robert, Percy, Violet, Iris and Ralph.

One of her sons was killed in the battle for the relief of Kimberley in the Boer War.

The 1881 Census records show that they had at that time twenty-one servants at Heythrop House, which included a governess/teacher from Mannheim in Germany.

She died in 1943.

On the right of the hall next to the door to the stage is a portrait of **James Houghton Langston Esq, MP** (1796–1863) of Sarsden House, which he inherited from his father in 1812 at the age of 16.

He became MP (Whig) for Woodstock and later Oxford City from 1826 until his death.

In 1818, he had Churchill Church rebuilt, with its tower modelled on Magdalen College, Oxford, and provided village schools in Lyneham, Milton-under-Wychwood and Chadlington.

He was described as "a kind and undeniable friend of the poor". He bred prize Longhorns and divided the 6,000 acre estate into a number of model farms whilst also providing allotments for tenants and workers.

Sarsden House was purchased by Lord Wyfold in 1920, and in 1995 by Shaun Woodward MP and his wealthy wife Camilla.

The house is now owned by Tony Gallagher, a property developer.

J.H. LANGSTON. Esq M.P
(OF SARSDEN)
WHO WAS LARGELY INSTRUMENTAL
IN THE ERECTION OF
THE CHIPPING NORTON TOWN HALL

On the upper landing is a document recording a joint accord with the French town *Magny-en-Vexin*, signed by Cllr D Roche and the Mayor of Magny.

At a Council meeting held on 5th June 1972, the Town Clerk reported that he had received a letter from Automotive Products, Banbury, concerning partnerships with towns in France and in particular Magny, and was asked to obtain more details.

At their meeting in November 1972, the Town Clerk reported that he had received correspondence from the Chairman of Amicale Magnytoise, a voluntary twinning association in the town of Magny-en-Vexin.

On 2nd April 1973, the Mayor Cllr Mrs Ethel Jackson held a public meeting with interested local organisations and Councillors and following this meeting twinning was started between Chipping Norton and Magny-en-Vexin. This continued with the new Mayor Cllr David Roche.

Exchange visits still take place, now as a Twinning Association; the Chairman is Keith Clandfield, and his wife Ann is the Secretary.

SERMENT
DE
JUMELAGE

Nous, Maires de Magny en Vexin – Chipping Norton

Librement désignés par le suffrage de nos concitoyens,

Certains de répondre aux aspirations profondes et aux besoins réels de nos populations,

Sachant que la civilisation occidentale a trouvé son berceau dans nos anciennes "communes" et que l'esprit de liberté s'est d'abord inscrit dans les franchises qu'elles surent conquérir,

Considérant que l'œuvre de l'histoire doit se poursuivre dans un monde élargi, mais que ce monde ne sera vraiment humain que dans la mesure où les hommes vivront libres dans des cités libres,

EN CE JOUR, NOUS PRENONS L'ENGAGEMENT SOLENNEL

- de maintenir des liens permanents entre les municipalités de nos communes, de favoriser en tous domaines les échanges entre leurs habitants pour développer, par une meilleure compréhension mutuelle, le sentiment vivant de la fraternité européenne,

- de conjuguer nos efforts afin d'aider dans la pleine mesure de nos moyens au succès de cette nécessaire entreprise de paix et de prospérité : **L'UNITÉ EUROPÉENNE**.

Fait à Magny en Vexin
Le 17 Mai 1975

The literal translation is as follows, although the text is rather formal. However, the gist is of a Twinning Charter.

S E R M O N
O F
T W I N N I N G

We, the Mayors of Magny-en-Vexin – Chipping Norton
Who were freely elected by our fellow-townspeople's vote, are
responding to our population's profound hopes and actual needs.

Knowing that the source of Western civilisation was found in our ancient "parishes" and that the spirit of liberty was first of all consistent with franchises, which these parishes had the competence to prevail.

Taking into account that this historical achievement must continue in an enlarged world, but this world will only be truly human insofar as men will live freely in free cities.

ON THIS DAY WE UNDERTAKE
THE SOLEMN AGREEMENT

- to maintain permanent links between the municipalities of our towns, to encourage all fields of exchanges between their inhabitants with the aim of developing, by way of improved mutual comprehension, the living feeling of European fraternity

- to unite our efforts in an attempt to facilitate to the best of our ability the success of this essential enterprise for peace and prosperity : **EUROPEAN UNITY**

Magny-en-Vexin,
17 May 1975

The copper shield (*above*) now hanging in the lower hall was also presented to the town and has the same date as the document 17th May 1975.

There is a further reminder of the twinning link with Magny-en-Vexin: a large map hangs in the passage downstairs, leading to the lower hall. Magny is in the top left of the map *(see photographs)*.

DEPARTEMENT DU VAL D'OISE

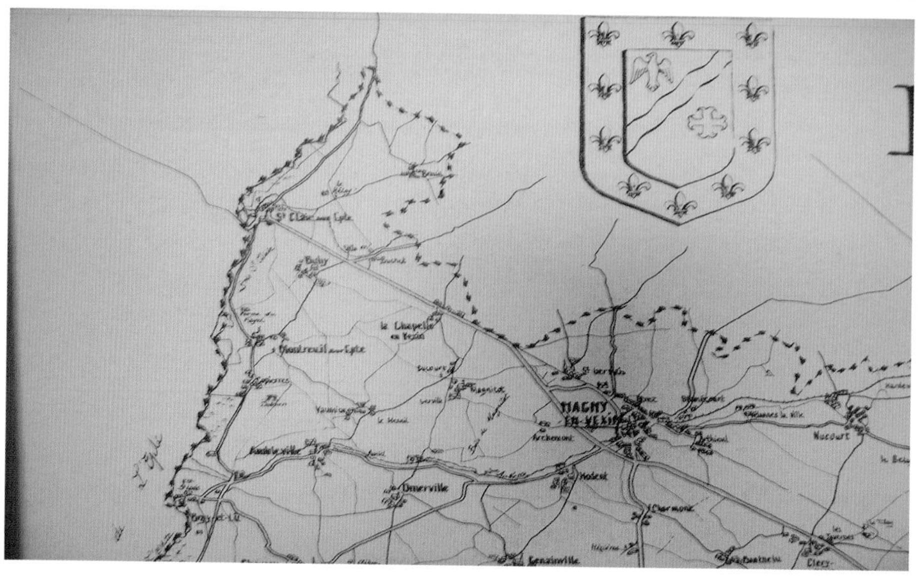

Below the Magny-en-Vexin twinning document is a drawing by a German PoW.

The plaque reads:

Chipping Norton Town Hall, 1947

Reproduced by kind permission of the author and presented by Cllr Robert Evans, Mayor 1995–6

Conrad Gries

Conrad Gries was a German prisoner of war housed at Greystones Camp, Chipping Norton, in 1946–7. As a young soldier, he was stationed on Alderney in the occupied Channel Islands. His main task was to make drawings of the minefields on Alderney as a military draughtsman and surveyor. During the liberation of the islands, the Germans ordered the destruction of the plans, and Conrad hid a second set in the hope that they would be found by the allies. He was captured in Jersey and helped in clearing the mines. The fact that there were only two fatalities on Alderney suggests that his drawings may have been discovered.

Conrad was then sent to Chipping Norton as a prisoner of war. Here he exercised his talents as an artist making several sketches of the town and surrounding area, some of which, like the one reproduced here, are in the possession of local families.

When it became possible for prisoners to be repatriated, Conrad spent several years working on the restoration of churches. Today, in semi-retirement, he is a partner in an art gallery in Herne, Germany. In 1988, Conrad and another PoW Erwin visited Greystones, Chipping Norton, but the Nissen huts have long since disappeared to accommodate its current use as a sports and recreation centre.

In 1990, by coincidence, he met Mr and Mrs Jack Brooks of Chipping Norton on a coaching tour of Scotland and interest in his early drawings of the town was renewed.

Also on the top landing is a painting of Chipping Norton Railway Station painted by Peter Sandels and presented to the Council.

Peter was a local boy, son of Harry Sandels, a builder, who lived in the large house in Horsefair now occupied by Chalford Blinds.

The builders yard was next door and the business was later taken over by Harry Bennett & Sons.

On the stairway near to the top landing is this plaque issued by the War Office in 1944:

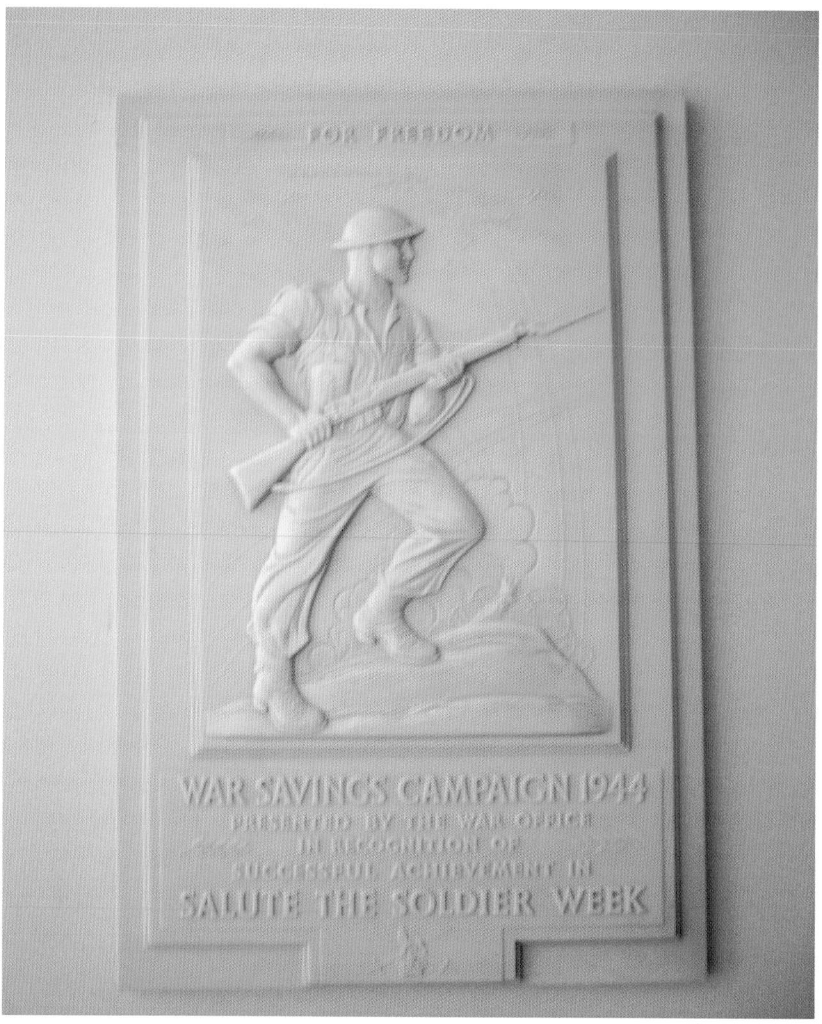

The four watercolours on the landing of the stairs were given in her will by Mrs Gwendoline Mary Walden (daughter of Frank Packer, Photographer) to Chipping Norton Town Council in 1999, on condition that they were displayed in the Town Hall, but not photographed or copied.

They are dated 1747 and are various views of the town before the first Enclosure in 1770.

These paintings used to hang in the passage of Packer's shop on High Street, and it was rumoured that they were given to Mr Frank Packer to clear an outstanding debt.

The watercolours were restored at the Oxfordshire County Council's Depository at Standlake at a cost of £1,270 by Michelle Bartlett (Restorer) and on her advice were hung in place on the landing to avoid direct sunlight.

As well as the large map of Magny, there are two other items housed in the downstairs passage leading to the lower hall.

The plaque shown above was presented to the town in 1966 and commemorates the 50th anniversary of National Savings.

The National Savings Organisation began in 1873 with the introduction of the Government Savings Bank Act. During the First World War many saving schemes were introduced for collection of funds to meet expenditure.

The other item is a framed copy of the 1770 Enclosure Award, produced by myself in 1985 as part of research into the history of common land in Chipping Norton.

Permission had been given by Messrs Farrant & Sinden (Solicitors) for the map, which at that time was in their office in Horsefair, to be copied. Using the Enclosure Award document, I amended and added the acreages not included in the original.

Having offered the amended version to the Council, the Mayor Cllr Tom Stroud invited me to present it formally to the Council at one of their meetings. This I did on 15th September 1986.

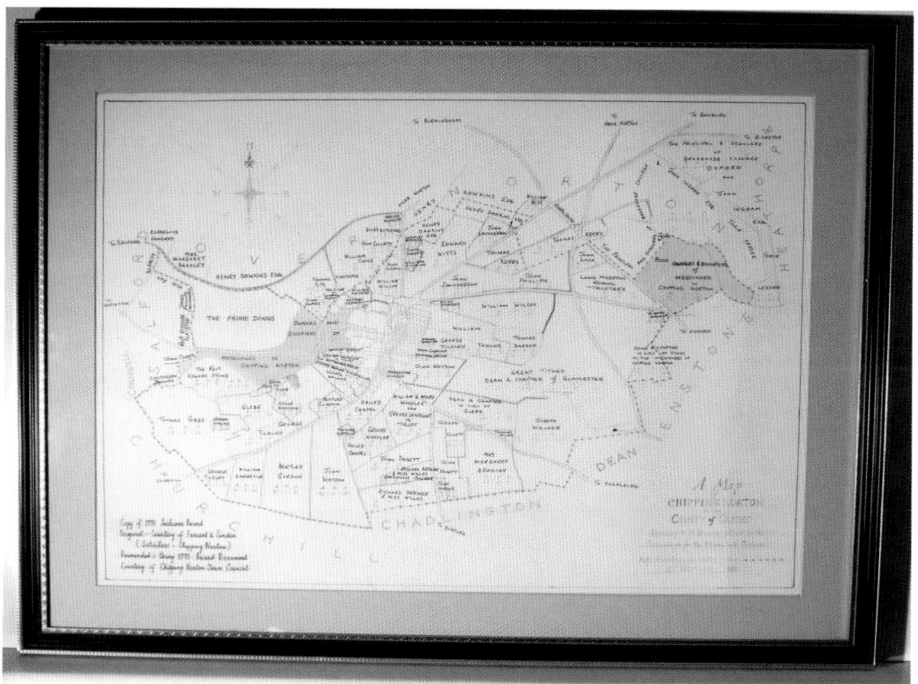

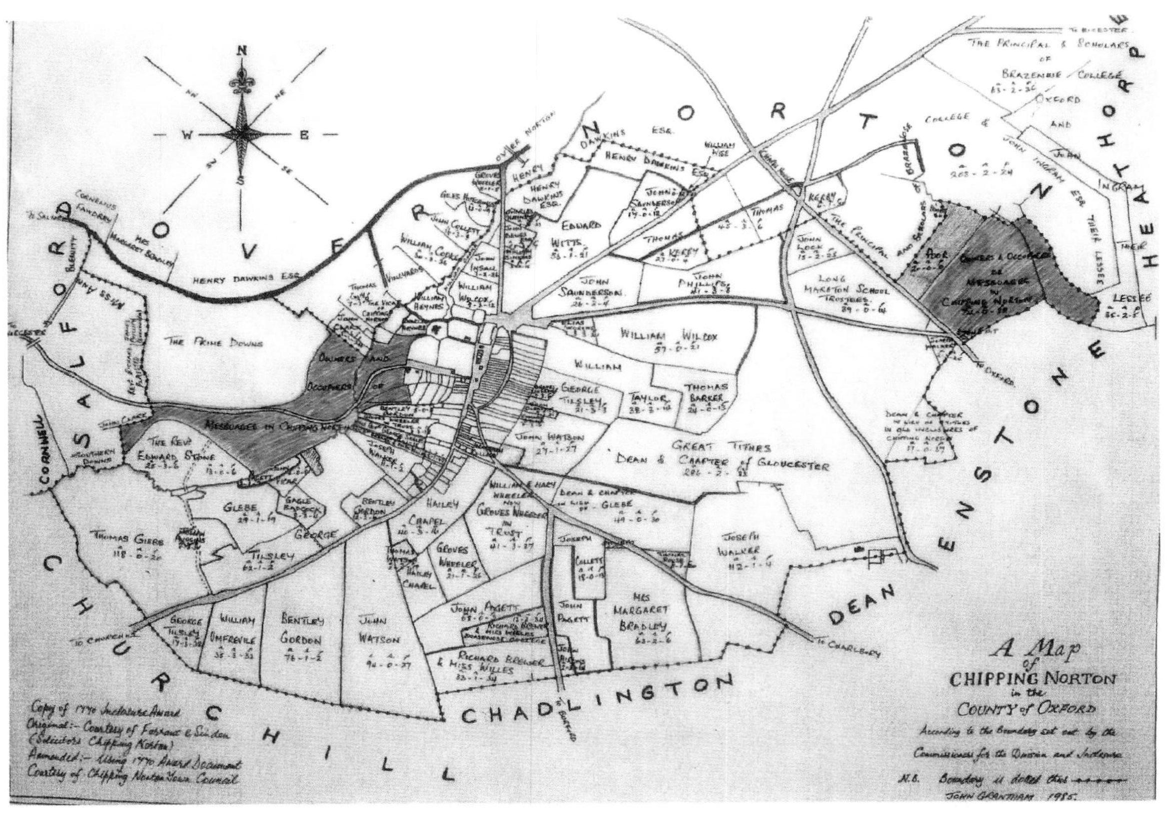

This photograph shows a more detailed version of my original drawing.

Information on other paintings and objects in the Lower Town Hall

Following the huge success of the War Weapons Week, Chipping Norton and Woodstock agreed to combine efforts again for Warships Week with the idea of formally adopting a ship for the district.

At first they thought in terms of a large minesweeper for which £136,000 would need to be raised. However, both towns were offered a Hunt class destroyer HMS Heythrop by the Admiralty.

The local association of the name naturally appealed but the district would have to set its sights much higher. For a town to adopt a destroyer, it was necessary for it to raise sufficient funds to pay for its hull – £150,000.

Chipping Norton and Woodstock districts however ambitiously decided on a target of £400,000 which represented the total cost of a new destroyer.

The President of the Committee was Lord Roche and the organisers included the Duke of Marlborough and the Mayor Mr Edgar Smith.

The week was arranged for 21st–28th March 1941.

A competition among school children for a slogan attracted 200 entries and was won by Olive Lewis of Churchill with the phrase:
"Save to defend and adopt a good friend—HMS Heythrop".

HMS Heythrop was built by Swan Hunter on the Tyne and completed in June 1941.

She was sent to Scapa Flow and then attached to the Irish Sea Escort Force of the Western Command. She was later transferred to the Mediterranean on escort duty until she was torpedoed and sunk by U-boats on 20th March 1942, with 49 fatal casualties, only five days after it was adopted.

The Chipping Norton area immediately resolved to save £180,000 within a month in order to convert their Warship Week total into the £400,000 required to replace the Heythrop with another destroyer.

The Admiralty were greatly encouraged by this decision and Chipping Norton became the first town in the country to organise a Warship Month.

The town was finally able to adopt another warship – HMS Magpie, a Black Swan Class Sloop, fitted with anti U-boat technology.

The Chipping Norton Borough and Rural District Council's received plaques from the Admiralty to commemorate their adoption of these two warships.

They are now displayed in the Lower Town Hall (*see below*).

The painting to the extreme left of the serving hatch is a view of the town as seen from an area near to Elmsfield Farm. It is difficult to read the artists name, but is signed
Hazel W Austin, Oxford, 1861.

Though not easy to see on the photograph, the painting shows, in the distance, the old windmill at the top of Rock Hill and the chimney of Hitchman's Brewery.

The painting also shows the upper Bliss Mill and the old Common Gate at the bottom of New Street before most the iron railings were installed.

Next to the left of the serving hatch is a large lithograph of the town centre, which has been reproduced many times both full size, in colour, and in smaller versions.

I have no idea who produced it; however, it is interesting to see the original arch at The White Hart Hotel. The attire of the people and carriages give a clue as to the period it depicts; I would guess c.1849–1860 but definitely not before, bearing in mind the Town Hall was built in 1842 and the clock and Bell Turret were not added until 1849.

In the lower hall next to the door leading to the Council Chamber is a photograph of Harold Leslie "Charlie" Withers.

Charlie Withers was elected to the Borough Council, attended his first meeting on 6th November 1946 and served continuously until he died on 21st July 1991. He was an Alderman in the Borough Council and also a Justice of the Peace. Although he would never accept the office of Mayor, in recognition of his long and loyal service to the town it was agreed his photograph would be displayed and would remain in the hall.

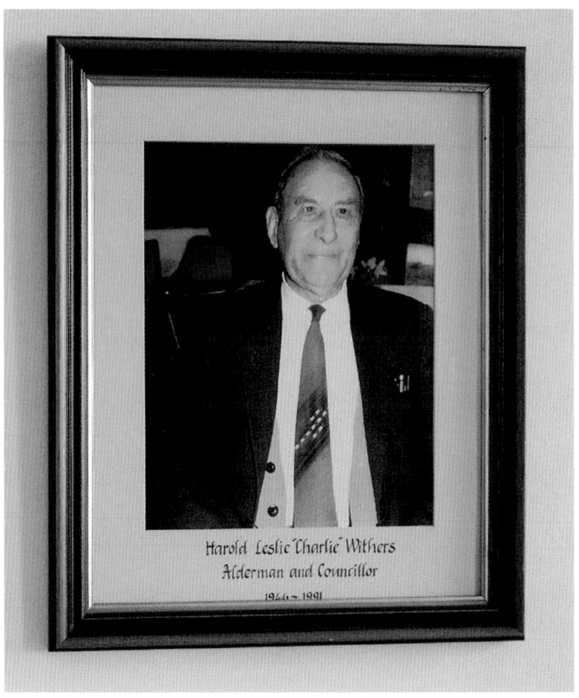

On the right-hand side of the door leading to the Council Chamber is a photograph of Hale-Bopp *, an unusually bright comet, over "The King Stone" near the Rollright Stone Circle, presented to the Council by Shaun Skeats, winner of the Millennium Photograph Competition.

*(* So called as on 23rd July 1995, this comet just outside Jupiter's orbit,was discovered independently by Alan Hale in New Mexico and Thomas Bopp in Arizona)*

Two large paintings are in the lower hall:

Thomas Mace, member of the Town Council 1874–1892, Mayor 1882/3 and 1887/8, Town Clerk 1892–1916. The painting was presented to the Borough by the Burgesses in 1911.

Alderman Charles Price Simms, a faithful member of Chipping Norton Town Council 1889–1907, painted in his 90th year. The painting presented to the Borough by the Burgesses in 1911.

The Council Chamber

The photograph shows the room as set up for Town Council meetings with the long table where Councillors sit.

The Mayor sits in the central large wooden chair, with the Deputy Mayor on the right and the Town Clerk on the left. Above on the left are names of past Mayors of the Borough Council, and on the right are names of past Mayors since being a Town Council.

The original boards are now in Chipping Norton Museum.

On the left side of the Chamber is a photograph of Her Majesty Queen Elizabeth II, signed by her on a visit to Chipping Norton on 8th April 1959. She was presented with a length of Bliss Tweed (*see photograph on page 91)*

The photograph was produced by Raphael Tuck & Sons, Fine Art Publishers.

COUNTY OF OXFORD

Visit of Her Majesty The Queen

8 APRIL 1959

In her tour of the County, Her Majesty will honour with personal visits each of the four Boroughs of Banbury, Chipping Norton, Henley-on-Thames, and Woodstock, and the Urban District of Witney. In the pages which follow details will be found of the programme, an introductory survey of the County, and a brief account of the main centres to be visited. Her Majesty will also pass through a number of parishes in the six Rural Districts of Banbury, Bullingdon, Chipping Norton, Henley, Ploughley, and Witney, whose ancient history and achievements cannot, for reasons of space, be recounted in these pages. It is regretted that time will not permit Her Majesty to visit, or even to pass through, the historic and thriving market towns which now comprise the Urban Districts of Bicester and Thame, but their local representatives will have the honour of being presented at other places on the tour

NORTON

The Council Chamber houses photographs of the most recent past Mayors who are still living.

Most of them are since the re-organisation of Local Government in 1974, when the town lost the majority of its powers to the newly created West Oxfordshire District Council. The two exceptions are Councillor John Gripper who was Mayor in 1966 and Councillor John Hannis who served in 1973. John Hannis was the last Mayor of the old Borough and the first person ever in Chipping Norton to be awarded the title "Honorary Citizen".

The system used to be that the outgoing Mayor's photograph was hung next to the portrait of Queen Elizabeth II and the other photographs were hung in order around the room.
If a Mayor died, and following a discreet period of time, the photograph was then removed from the chamber and stored.

Today, because of space, the system has been revised, and all the deceased past Mayors' photographs go to the Chipping Norton Museum to be on permanent display.

The Town Hall continues to be well used and still plays an important role in the life of the town. However, there are signs that large sums of money will soon need to be found to replace the sash windows and carry out restoration work on the exterior of the building.

Acknowledgements

Oxfordshire County Record Office
Chipping Norton Town Council
Mr Michael Fletcher (Former Town Clerk)
Mrs Vanessa Oliveri (Town Clerk)
Mrs Janet Griffin (Guildhall Staff)
Mr Terry Palmer (Town Hall Keeper)
Mr John Hannis
Mr John Brice
Mr David Nobbs
Mr Alexander Corfield
Dr's Bruce & Sheila Parker
Chipping Norton Museum, for allowing me to copy documents from their archive.
Mr Alan Brain, for allowing me to use rare bankers slips and five photographs from his collection.

Mlle Vivienne Hunt, for the correct translation of the Magny-en-Vexin document.

Mr R L Evans & Mrs G M Burrows, who provided some of the original information on various photographs and items.

The late Mr Frank Packer, for most of the older photographs which I have used, and are in my collection.

Mr Adam Robson, for his invaluable technical support, and
Mrs Rosemary Osmond for proof reading and editing the book

Miss Lauren Grantham (My 14 year old Granddaughter), for her help in planning and arranging the layout of this book.